The Holy Grail of

A Modern Strategy fo

Charlie Cazalet

Illustrations by Charles Gouldsbrough

MLC Publishing

First published in the UK in 2015 by MLC Publishing

ISBN: 978-0-9933287-0-1

A CIP catalogue record for this book is available from the British Library.

Printed and bound in Great Britain by
CPI Group (UK) Ltd
Croydon
CR0 4YY

MLC Publishing
38 Norland Square
London
W11 4PZ

Typeset in Minion Pro

About the Author

Charlie Cazalet was born in London, UK, in 1987. He sat his GCSEs in 2003-2004 and his AS/A-Levels in 2005-2006. In 2007, he began a four-year BA degree in French & Italian at the University of Bristol, UK, spending 5 months each at the Universities of Aix-Marseille I and Verona during his third year abroad. He graduated in 2011 and went on to complete his formal education with two years at BPP Law School, UK, in 2013-2014, receiving a Distinction grade in his final exams.

Charlie is a keen photographer (www.charliecazalet.com), freeskier, electric guitarist, golfer, footballer and fitness enthusiast.

With thanks to Amy, Andrei, Anthony, Charles, Frederick, Harry and my family for your opinions and suggestions.

Contents

Introduction

Do you enjoy exams? I doubt it. Unfortunately we all have to sit them at some stage in our education. They creep up on us and question our ability to act under pressure. Exams have become an essential means of qualification and, if you haven't already, you'll have to get used to them. If you're reading this then chances are you've got some coming up soon. You're possibly unsure how to approach them. In fact, you may well be dreading them. You might even have convinced yourself that you'll fail. Do yourself a favour and put all these thoughts aside. Now read on.

From what I can make out, most exam-orientated publications are written either by teachers who sat their 'O-Levels' in the 1970s, memory champions to whom few of us can ever begin to relate or precocious child geniuses. I want you to relax in the realization that I'm none of these things. I sat my GCSEs in 2003-2004 (similar to a US high school diploma), my AS/A-Levels in 2005-2006 (similar to Advanced Placement exams/ SATs in the US, Year 12 study exams in Australia, 12th Boards in India and the Gaokao in China), my university finals in 2011 and two years of legal exams in 2013-2014. I've been taking exams since before I can remember.

As exams required more work, so my approach to them began to shift. I realized that there's more to preparing for exams than meets the eye, but at the same time, the claim that I had heard so frequently repeated over the years that 'exams are more about understanding than memorization' continued to frustrate me. Perhaps the powers that be have some sort of romanticised ideal about why we're taking exams, but the long and short of it remains the same: while a comprehensive understanding of a subject is the essence of a perfect education, in reality, most exams are ultimately a test of regurgitating information or techniques that have been memorized. While this is possibly a grim indictment on any country's educational system, every student knows that this is the case.

Now I want to make it absolutely clear that this book is not some sort of memorization shortcut. There are numerous self-help books available, both in print and eBook format, which purport to be able to teach you how to memorize staggering quantities of information in record time. You know they exist; you might even have bought one. They look highly appealing – who wouldn't want to be able to do what they can supposedly promise? However, I can tell you from experience that while some of the techniques in these publications can be useful, it takes time and a great deal of practice to get any benefit from them – both of which I recognize you most likely don't have.

By contrast, this book will take an alternative, holistic approach to exam preparation. I've bought and used a number of well-known books on how to pass exams over the years, and I've regularly been frustrated to find that while the information contained within many of them is sound, all too often the techniques used are simply a variation on a theme: one that revolves primarily around study techniques. Now, in no way do I not recognize the importance of good study technique; indeed, I will dedicate a chapter to it. Nevertheless, what I've come to understand is that, before a person can study effectively, there are other significant factors that need to be taken into account. These, I believe, have almost universally been ignored up until now, and in reality the opposite should be the case.

Therefore, before I even begin to discuss how to study effectively and sit an exam, I want us to consider three other crucial interrelated factors that are just as important, if not far more important, than the preparation and the exam itself.

How to Use the Information in this Book

In an ideal world you'll have bought this some time before you have to sit an exam. If you only have a few days until your exams, then take what you can, but I can't promise miracles. If, on the other hand, you have two to six weeks (or longer) until your exams, depending, of course, on the difficulty of the papers that you'll be sitting, then congratulate yourself for planning ahead and please put my ideas to good use.

There are many other self-help exam books out there with hundreds of pages of difficult-to-remember tips and tricks. This book, however, is different. I would hope that you might be able to finish it quickly in one or two sittings, and thereafter have it by your side and use it as a reference whenever you need to be reminded of what I suggest. It's intended to be short and succinct. There are no gimmicks and no complex memory tricks. Instead, my approach is a collection of the very best bits that I've gathered from current science, scholarly articles and institutions and, above all, my own personal experience. I'm confident that everybody can benefit from what I have to recommend, so please try to embrace my ideas, even if at first they may seem unusual.

Finally, I hope it goes without saying that deciding

to use just *some* bits of what I suggest will not necessarily be effective. You might decide that a slightly different study method works better for you, and there's nothing wrong with that. However, to get the maximum out of this information, I advise that you apply the underlying foundations of what I propose as closely as possible.

NB. In the UK, we use the words *revise* and *revision* in the context of exam preparation. In the USA, Australia and elsewhere, these words have a different meaning and are used instead in the context of creating a new version of a piece of coursework, for example, through editing and rewriting. In the interests of making this book understandable for all students, I've taken the decision to use the word *study* in relation to exam preparation, since this is a word that we can all understand.

1. The Power of Sleep

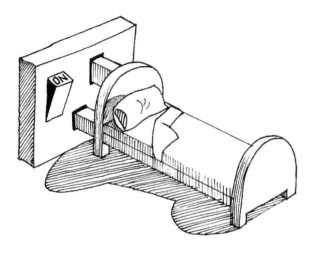

If there's one thing that you should take away from this book, let it be the fact that there's nothing more essential to your quest for exam success than a good night's sleep. Absolutely nothing.

Now, I bet you're thinking that you've heard this one before, and you may think you know better, but please stop and read on. Science has caught up with sleep-deprived students and there's now firm evidence to indicate that going to bed at the wrong time or denying yourself sleep are having a far greater impact on you than you might imagine. There's an old saying that "an hour before midnight is worth two after", and it would seem that whoever coined that phrase hit the jackpot.

The Body's Internal Clock & Efficient Sleep

Scientists have known for some time that the human body runs on a 24-hour cycle, often referred to by you and I as our 'body clock', and by scientists as the 'circadian rhythm'. It has now been shown that the best sleep is achieved when your circadian rhythm is at its lowest ebb, in other words, between around 10pm and 5am.

It follows that even if you think you've had a good night's sleep (anything from seven to nine hours), this may not be the case. For example, let's say you went to bed at 1am and woke at 8am, achieving what seems like a decent seven hours' sleep. This might appear adequate, but the reality is that you're not capitalising on the benefits that you could be reaping from keeping your sleep in tune with your body's biological process. In short, your sleep is inefficient.

Therefore, to get the maximum out of your time in bed, try to go to sleep well before midnight. I recommend that you start to prepare for bed around 10:30pm at the latest, and then hit the hay shortly after. That way you get a good hour before midnight, and your body can profit from at least six hours when it's benefiting most from the rest. Aim to then wake at 7am or earlier.

I am myself something of a night owl and I stress that this is not the way I would normally operate either. However, please believe me when I tell you that there's no more powerful weapon in your arsenal than bringing your usual bedtime back a few hours. It will pay dividends.

While inevitably computers, phones and tablets seem to have taken their toll on our lives and keep the human brain ticking over and wired-in at all times, help yourself by switching off your laptop and putting your phone on silent some time before bed. A cool, dark room with no disturbances should help you on your way to achieving this first aim of a good night's sleep.

Mood, Stress & Memory

So why have I placed such emphasis on sleeping efficiently? The answer to this is threefold and of the utmost importance to you.

Firstly, we all know that on the occasion that you might have slept particularly well, come the following morning you can feel on top of the world. Nothing can stop you, you're in the zone and you couldn't be in a better mood. Efficient sleep has the power to make you feel this good every single day. Your learning and ability to recall information will benefit exponentially from an increased ability to concentrate and a positive attitude to doing so.

Secondly, during the period of sleep known as 'rapid eye movement' sleep (REM), this is the only time of day (or night) when one of the chemicals linked to stress in the brain, 'noradrenalin', is *not* produced. An efficient night's sleep will help promote REM sleep, thereby reducing the stress that you're feeling in the run-up to exams.

Lastly and most crucially of all, recent scientific evidence has begun to show the significance of the role that sleep plays in managing and consolidating memories in the human brain. Learning and remembering information is often referred to as three distinct processes:

- Acquisition – the absorption of information
- Consolidation – the solidification of that information into a memory
- Recall – the ability to access memories

Both 'acquisition' and 'recall' only occur while you're awake, but research would appear to show that 'consolidation' takes place during sleep. By a process which still remains little understood, many scientists now believe that sleep allows connections between neurons in the human brain to strengthen, resulting in memory consolidation. Therefore, it should come as no surprise that high-quality, efficient sleep should accordingly help boost your brain's capacity for remembering and retaining information. From personal experience this is undoubtedly the case and, since this is the key to exam success, nothing should be a higher priority for you right now than getting a good night's sleep. And, if that isn't strong enough proof for you, researchers at Harvard Medical School have shown that if a person learns something and then sleeps on it, on waking they can be up to 10 times better at doing it than if they had remained awake!

As a final afterthought, you may have sometimes wondered how dreams fit in to the bigger picture. Research now seems to show that dreams are the physical manifestation of the consolidation of our memories. I personally have found during times when I was absorbing large amounts of information on a daily basis, for example before my university finals or legal exams, that my dreams were extraordinarily vivid compared to normal, so this may be a perfect example of memory consolidation in action in my own brain.

Summary

- Prepare for bed at 10:30pm (or earlier) and wake no later than 7am to achieve around 8 hours of efficient sleep that coincides with the lowest ebb of your body clock (between 10pm and 5am).

- Efficient sleep will:

  1. Improve concentration and attitudes to study
  2. Reduce exam stress
  3. Enhance your brain's ability to absorb and retain information

- Be mindful of any vivid dreams, a possible indication of memory consolidation in action.

Further Reading

- http://healthysleep.med.harvard.edu
- http://learnmem.cshlp.org
- http://sleepfoundation.org
- http://www.sleephealthfoundation.org.au

2. Food for Thought

In 1825, Jean Anthelme Brillat-Savarin, the father of modern food writing, wrote in his famous work, *The Physiology of Taste*, "Tell me what you eat, and I will tell you what you are." Brillat-Savarin had made the crucial link between food and a healthy mind. What to eat, how to eat and when to eat is collectively a subject that today seems almost exclusively the preserve of dieting books and weight-loss programmes. But it shouldn't be. We only sleep for around one third of a 24-hour day; therefore the food and drink that we consume will provide us with the energy that we need to tackle the other two thirds of the day that we spend awake. As we now know, sleep plays the principal role in managing our mood and our capacity for learning during the day, but it's the food and drink that we consume which will then dictate how the body can best maximise the benefits of this sleep.

I make no excuse for this chapter's being the most brutal to adapt to. What I'm going to suggest may prove challenging for a number of reasons. You might not like the foods that I propose you eat, you might be resistant to the idea of giving up those things that you've always relied on to give you a boost when you needed it, or you might think that the extra cost doesn't justify the end result, especially if your student loan is starting to dwindle. I understand that we're all different when it comes to food and drink and that we have our own personal preferences, but please try to follow my advice as closely as possible. Above all, really do avoid those things that I clearly indicate will do you no good at all!

Blood Sugar Levels

Trial and error has shown me that the key to remaining focused all day long lies in sustaining your energy levels. This does not mean maintaining some sort of daily high by starting the morning off with a liquid breakfast of coffee, followed by a diet of chocolate bars, toast and yet more coffee (college/university students take note). Instead, it means beginning the day with a high-quality breakfast, and then maintaining relatively uniform blood sugar levels throughout the day by eating to a consistent schedule and snacking healthily when need be. I don't expect that you've often thought about your blood sugar (or glucose) level (unless, of course, you're diabetic), but its effects can be profound when it comes to your mood and, by association, your capacity to concentrate.

Think, for a moment, about the last time that you ate a low-quality sugary chocolate bar. The almost instant buzz of energy it gave you was exactly what you were looking for, correct? Now think of the period a little after you ate that bar. You might not have been looking out for it, but I can guarantee that you'll have felt a slight drop in energy, and perhaps a significant one if that bar was the only thing you had eaten for some time. The reason for this is that by eating the chocolate bar you're abnormally spiking your blood sugar levels. This will result in your body releasing insulin (a hormone) to counteract the heightened levels of glucose in your blood. The end consequence is a rapid absorption of glucose into your body's tissues, where it will either be used to create energy or stored by your body. This rapid absorption of glucose and the subsequent fall in the level of glucose in your blood results in what people often call a 'sugar crash'. Such a crash will make you feel moody, lazy and unproductive, and may even cause you to feel anxious or give you a headache. This is evidently precisely what we're trying to avoid, so with that in mind, let's now focus on the kinds of food and drink that will both help and hinder successful exam preparation.

Food & Drink to Fuel the Mind

You should try to introduce the following foods and drinks into your daily diet and, where I recommend it, eat or drink them every day. Nevertheless, I'm keen to stress that consuming what I suggest will *not* turn you into a genius overnight! What it will do, however, is give your body and brain the best possible chance to function at their optimal capacity and, if the studies and science are correct, then it may well be that you'll receive the added benefits that they profess to prove. I haven't listed every possible healthy food and drink that I could research, but rather a shorter list of the most essential 'brain foods' that are both easy enough to find in local supermarkets and which should benefit you the most.

Please note that in no way do I have an association

with any food brand mentioned. If I do mention a brand, I'm simply trying to point out which is the best in terms of quality and taste in my experience.

Water – This might seem the most obvious thing on this list, but we simply do not drink enough water! Up to 60% of the human body is made up of water. Our brains need a combination of nutrients *and* water to function optimally and dehydration can impair your ability to concentrate, perform calculations, and most importantly, the functioning of your short and long-term memory.

While we breathe, we continually exhale water vapour, so when you wake in the morning, start the day by drinking a glass or two of water to rehydrate your body and brain. Thereafter, keep a glass or bottle of water by your side at ALL times and drink continually throughout the day. A good average to aim for is around two litres of water per day. I cannot stress more how essential water is!

Blueberries – These little fruits are known as a true superfood. Not only do they taste delicious, but they also contain a remarkable number of benefits. They're a good source of Vitamin K (blood clotting, strong bones, cognitive function), Vitamin C (healthy cells &

tissue, immune system), fibre (digestive health, heart health), manganese (healthy bones), and flavonoids (antioxidants). There's also a growing body of evidence to support a link with improved learning, memory and cognitive function.

Blueberries are particularly versatile and can be eaten with breakfast, lunch or dinner, or as a healthy snack. I propose that you try to eat a punnet a day. Look out for smaller blueberries in packs – I find these to be the best tasting and most crunchy. While you might baulk at the daily £2/$3 price tag, be conscious of the fact that this diet is only for as many weeks as you're preparing for your exams. What's more, those things that you'll no longer be eating should help to offset the small additional cost.

Apples – No wonder an apple a day keeps the doctor away as they contain an impressive range of benefits: Vitamin C, fibre, a range of minerals including boron (bone health, disease prevention) and potassium (heart health), and flavonoids. The latter is said to be able to help the body regulate its blood sugar levels.

As the rhyme dictates, I advise that you do indeed eat an apple a day. Personally, I love the 'Pink Lady' variety (sorry, UK farmers). It's worth finding your favourite when it's a daily staple.

Bananas – These are going to take the place of the sweets and chocolate that you used to eat. Bananas are a source of fibre, magnesium (brain function), Vitamin B6 (cognitive function), and amino acids (mood control). They're also an excellent source of glucose in the form of fructose (fruit sugar). This natural sugar is released more slowly into the bloodstream than the refined sugar (sucrose) found in cakes and sweets, providing your brain with the consistent supply of energy that it requires for optimal functioning.

Freshly squeezed orange juice (with the juicy bits) – Like me, you may find that peeling an orange, removing the pith and then eating messy segments can seem like more effort than just munching an apple. Freshly squeezed orange juice solves this problem and ensures that while you won't get any of the benefit of the fibre in a whole orange, you do maximise your intake of Vitamin C, magnesium, flavonoids and minerals, all of which it contains in abundance. You can buy it at most decent supermarkets and I recommend that you have a single glass every morning with your breakfast to get the day started.

Spinach – One of the kings of the vegetable world, spinach might not make you as strong as Popeye, but it will certainly do your body and brain good. This leafy green contains a broad range of benefits including Vitamin A (healthy eye function, immune system), Vitamin K, Vitamin C, Vitamin E (antioxidant properties), and high levels of Vitamin B9 (aka folate), which plays a significant role in healthy brain function.

Cooking spinach is said to actually improve its benefits owing to the fact that the human body struggles to break down raw spinach and is therefore unable to take advantage of all of its nutrients. In any case, whether raw or cooked, spinach is an excellent choice, and I recommend eating it with either your lunch or dinner every day.

Broccoli – Another potent vegetable, broccoli contains Vitamin C and K and, like spinach, is a good source of Vitamin B9. It's also high in a nutrient called choline that studies show may improve cognitive function, especially in relation to memory. Like spinach, I advise eating a decent sized portion daily and eat both the florets (tops) and the stems (the sweetest, tastiest bits).

Fish (oily) – Oily fish include salmon, mackerel, tuna, anchovies and sardines (among others). These fish are rich in Vitamin D (healthy bones) and long-chain omega-3 fatty acids, and should be bought fresh, not tinned, where possible. Numerous studies have been carried out investigating a potential link between omega-3 and improved heart and/or brain function. Suffice to say there's now strong evidence to indicate that omega-3 helps protect against cardiovascular disease, but the exact effect of omega-3 on the brain remains less well understood. However, what have been proven definitively are the significant overall health benefits of eating oily fish and a link to improved cognitive function and memory, even if the scientists can't say exactly why.

So I advise that you try to eat around two to three portions of oily fish per week. What's more, don't let me stop you eating other 'non-oily' white fish such as cod, haddock, sea bass etc. These fish are by far preferable to a diet of pizza and ready meals, contain many nutrients and health benefits, and are much more digestible (particularly before bed). Go to your local fishmonger or supermarket fish counter to find the best value deals (as opposed to buying pre-packaged fish off the shelves which is overpriced) – some fish such as mackerel cost very little indeed. Bake or grill (as opposed to frying) the above to preserve their benefits.

Eggs – Another superfood, eggs contain a complete range of nutrients and vitamins that are too diverse to list in full here. In particular, they're an important source of choline (see Broccoli) and have high levels of protein, within which many of the essential amino acids are contained and which benefit the body as well as the brain.

I recommend having one or two eggs every morning with your breakfast, however you like them. I personally prefer a quick omelette, but boiled eggs might be the easiest option.

Quinoa – A little known seed that tastes like a cross between couscous and rice but which is technically a legume, quinoa is a staple in the diets of many South American peoples. It's a superfood in the true sense of the word, being very high in protein (amino acids) and fibre, and also having a very low-glycaemic index. This means that it will digest and release its energy more slowly.

Quinoa takes about 20 minutes to cook in boiling water, but a large batch can be made and it can then be eaten cold with subsequent meals. It makes a perfect alternative to rice or couscous, and a far healthier one too. It's not always easy to find in supermarkets (though increasingly becoming easier), but health food shops will generally stock it, and a bag goes a long way (the seeds expand considerably in size on cooking).

Sweet potatoes – While not classically recognized as a brain food, sweet potatoes contain a surprisingly diverse range of vitamins and minerals. They make for an excellent change to regular potatoes, which are also a great source of carbohydrate-based energy. Sweet potatoes contain high levels of Vitamin A. They're also a good source of Vitamin C, Vitamin B6, manganese and potassium. Steam, boil or bake.

Muesli – In terms of breakfast cereals, muesli with *no added sugar* or other nasty additions is key here. The wholegrains in muesli also have a low-glycaemic index (see above). Brands of cereal that you're probably more familiar with often contain added sugar and other ingredients that you *do not* need. Good marketing has made cereals such as cornflakes and others appear attractive and, while these will provide you with *some* goodness, this pales in comparison to the benefits of eating muesli rich in wholegrains and nuts.

I've personally observed that a muesli-based breakfast can provide me with enough energy to almost always keep me going right through until the end of the morning, whereas I'd often be feeling positively flat around 10:30am having eaten an equivalent sized bowl of cornflakes. Try it for yourself – you'll be amazed at the difference! I recommend in particular 'Simply

Delicious Muesli' by the brand Dorset Cereals here in the UK – if you've ever thought of muesli as a boring or tasteless cereal, their excellent range of regular or nut based, no-added-sugar muesli will be sure to change your mind. Be well aware, however, that many types of muesli *do* have added sugar, so take extra care to find a brand that does *not*.

Nuts & seeds (unsalted) – Cashews, pistachios, peanuts, almonds, hazelnuts, walnuts, sunflower seeds, sesame seeds, pine nuts and pumpkin seeds (among others) all make the perfect snack in between meals. Walnuts in particular get an honourable mention here, containing Vitamin E, Vitamin B6 and omega-3 and 6 fatty acids. Overall, the above nuts and seeds are a good source of Vitamin E and are packed with essential fats that provide high levels of energy relative to their small size.

Fill a bowl with a mixture of nuts and seeds to snack on late in the morning before lunch. It goes without saying that if you have any concerns about nut allergies then please consult your doctor before eating any of the nuts listed above.

Supplements – Sometimes bandied around as a shortcut to good health, these include the likes of Vitamin C tablets, multivitamins and omega-3 capsules. While these may prove beneficial, if you're eating a diet full of those foods that I've already suggested above, there shouldn't be any need for extra supplements. That being said, taking one Vitamin C tablet + zinc per day (the zinc aids absorption) is a possible option, and although scientists are still researching the effects of omega-3 on the brain as previously mentioned, if you feel like it might give yours a boost then by all means take one daily. Even if it's actually doing very little, the psychosomatic effect might be worth it.

In addition to those foods listed above, I propose the following to complement a diet that will keep your body and brain in the best possible shape: avocados, tomatoes, peppers, carrots, green beans, mushrooms, potatoes, kiwi fruits, lemons, limes, blackcurrants, blackberries, grapes, passion fruits, chicken, wholegrain brown rice, wholegrain bread and extra virgin olive oil.

Food & Drink to Avoid

Cakes, biscuits, sweets & chocolate – These foods contain high levels of refined sugar (sucrose). They'll lift you up on a sugar high and then send you crashing back down (see 'Blood Sugar Levels' above). Foods such as these will impact your concentration, mood and general productivity, and are to be avoided at all costs.

It should be noted that there's a growing body of evidence showing that 'dark' chocolate may in fact be beneficial for circulation in the human body in small amounts. So, if you're craving something sweet, why not have a small piece along with some berries as part of your dessert at dinner. Dark chocolate means any chocolate having a percentage of cocoa solids of more than 70%.

Fruit juices, squash & smoothies – Most fruit juices and squash (and especially those from concentrate) are high in sugar, so try to avoid them and favour one glass per day of freshly squeezed orange juice instead. Be well aware, however, that freshly squeezed orange juice is itself still high in sugar! Although smoothies purport to provide goodness, much of that has been lost in the blending process, and they, likewise, are very high in sugar.

Alcohol – For those of you that are above the legal age limit to drink, I would strongly advise that you try to cut out all alcohol for the duration of your exam preparation. While there may be peer pressure to stay on the booze, people generally seem to understand when you say that you're preparing for important exams, and fellow students who are also taking exams may well follow your lead when you tell them the benefits of going teetotal.

Clearly trying to study with a hangover is a recipe for disaster, so this is one good reason to avoid alcohol in the evenings. Additionally, although evidence is somewhat mixed as to what effect alcohol will have on your memory, it's a scientific fact that alcohol causes dehydration (through inhibition of the anti-diuretic hormone (ADH)) and that it leads to disturbed sleep patterns. Since proper hydration and a good night's sleep are both crucial to our cause, alcohol should therefore be avoided. In response to my advice, a friend coined the phrase "punnets over pints". Be sure to remember it.

Coffee & tea – This is one of the more controversial recommendations that I will make, since I'm well aware that many people reading this (especially university/college students) will regularly rely on the caffeine (and possibly sugar) in these drinks to keep them going at all times of the day. The problem with caffeine before or during study is firstly that, like alcohol, it's a diuretic and therefore results in dehydration. The second problem is that it's a stimulant that triggers the release of hormones such as adrenaline and cortisol. Adrenaline will lift you up initially, but later you'll probably feel tired and possibly even depressed, and cortisol is known as the 'stress hormone'. And, if the above aren't enough to persuade you away from caffeine, all of these factors will, like alcohol, lead to disturbed sleep patterns.

The good news is that if you start your day with the breakfast that I propose, there'll be no need for any caffeine in the morning and, since you won't be working beyond a certain hour of the day, there'll equally be no need for caffeine to keep you awake into the early hours. Caffeine, therefore, becomes unnecessary. I advise that you stop drinking coffee and/or tea some weeks in advance of any exam preparation period to help avoid any possible caffeine withdrawal symptoms (headaches, anxiety, fatigue etc.). This is especially true if you're usually partial to a number of cups per day.

Fizzy drinks – These are packed with sugar and in some cases caffeine so, for the same reasons as above, avoid them at all costs. 'Diet' variants of many fizzy drinks should equally be avoided. Despite the fact that on the face of it a 'diet' drink may contain no calories, it is in fact made up of a cocktail of chemicals, including artificial sweeteners, which your body will react to in the same way as if you were consuming refined sugar in a regular fizzy drink.

Energy drinks – There are many different brands on the market and some are backed by huge marketing campaigns. Don't be swayed by the claims. Energy drinks are crammed with caffeine and sugar, and in terms of study as we now know, this is a lethal combination.

A Working Day's Menu

The menu overleaf shows how easy it is to incorporate many of the brain foods that I recommend into your daily intake. Whereas from experience it's best if the same breakfast is eaten every day (with minor alterations which are up to you), feel free to vary what you eat for lunch or dinner. You'll probably get pretty fed up of having eggs every morning by the time your exams are done, but it really is worth it! Crucially, avoid heavy, rich or spicy meals with red meat, rice, cream or cheese in the evening. This means that curries, steaks, burgers, pizzas, crème brûlée and similar are all off the menu. Foods such as these don't digest easily and may result in your sleep patterns being disrupted.

Breakfast

- Infusion (e.g. lemon & ginger or fresh mint), to take the place of the coffee or tea that you might otherwise drink
- Glass of freshly squeezed orange juice
- Bowl of muesli with semi-skimmed milk
- Two egg omelette

Morning Snack

- Apple
- Bowl of nuts & seeds

Lunch

- Salmon
- Quinoa
- Spinach
- Tomatoes
- Blueberries

Afternoon Snack

- Banana

Dinner

- Chicken breast
- Sweet potato
- Broccoli
- Green beans
- Blackberries & raspberries

Clearly not everybody is in a position to eat such a healthy meal every day for lunch and dinner for numerous reasons, but there's no excuse whatsoever for not getting up in good enough time to allow yourself a full breakfast. This is without doubt the most vital meal of the day when you're studying and is a major element in the success that you're seeking.

Lastly, I fully expect that some people might question what may seem like the additional cost of changing your eating habits. I suggest that you think about this in a different way. Consider for a moment what you'll now no longer be eating and drinking (cakes, sweets, chocolate bars, pizzas, crisps, fizzy drinks, alcohol, expensive take-away coffees etc.) and then realize that the cost of eating healthily should most likely be offset by the cost savings that you're making in terms of avoiding the above. And, if you do find that your shopping bill has increased a little, then surely good exam grades are worth a few extra pounds/dollars per week?

Summary

- Keep well hydrated by drinking water throughout the day.

- Start the day with a wholesome breakfast of freshly squeezed orange juice, a bowl of muesli and 1 or 2 eggs. Repeat daily.

- Maintain glucose levels throughout the day by eating healthy snacks and balanced meals made up of 'brain food' ingredients such as blueberries, apples, bananas, spinach, broccoli, oily fish, quinoa, and nuts and seeds.

- Avoid sugary foods and drinks, alcohol and caffeine at all costs.

- Avoid rich/heavy meals in the evening before bed.

Further Reading

- http://water.usgs.gov/edu/propertyyou.html
- http://nutritiondata.self.com
- https://www.drinkaware.co.uk/check-the-facts

3. Exercising the Mind

This third pillar of my approach to exam preparation success is easier to implement, doesn't have to cost anything if you don't want it to, and simply requires a bit of your time and commitment. Your brain, like your body, will benefit greatly from physical exercise. I'm briefly going to explain why this is and suggest a few ideas to keep you active. Try to exercise as frequently as possible and mix it up from day to day. Lastly, this chapter is clearly shorter because there's only a limited amount of explanation needed in this particular area.

Brain

Physical exercise and above all aerobic exercise (aka 'cardiovascular' exercise), which gets your heart beating fast, results in more oxygen being pumped to the brain. Research by UCLA has shown that only a small amount of exercise over a few days can result in the growth of new neural connections and thereby an increase in the plasticity of the brain. A study by the University of Georgia has also shown that exercising for only 20 minutes can improve memory function.

Mood

Exercise results in an increase in blood calcium that in turn stimulates the release of the hormone dopamine. Dopamine is responsible for making you feel energised and happy. Accordingly, if you're in a good mood, you'll probably be more productive. By contrast, low levels of dopamine will make you feel tired and depressed.

Sleep

The relationship between sleep and exercise is surprising and more significant than you might have realized. When you're nearing the time for bed, you won't have ever been aware, but your body is actually signalling this by slightly dropping in temperature. Then, as you sleep, your body remains at this slightly lower temperature (compared to when you're awake), reaching its coolest in the early hours of the morning before sunrise.

When you exercise aerobically, the temperature of your body will actually increase slightly. 20 to 30 minutes of good exercise will mean that your body stays at this slightly elevated temperature for the next four to five hours after you've finished exercising, before dropping back to its normal level.

Therefore, given both of the above, if you can time it so that your workout *ends* around four to five hours before you go to bed, i.e. between 6pm and 7pm, you'll then be able to benefit from your body's increase and subsequent eventual post-exercise drop in temperature matching the natural drop in your body's temperature before sleep. By doing so, it has been shown that particularly deep, sound sleep can be achieved. From personal experience, this is undoubtedly the case.

Be aware that conversely, exercising just before bed will have an adverse effect and make it more difficult for you to fall asleep. And lastly, if you only have the time to exercise in the morning, fear not, because doing so will still have a positive effect on your mood and stress levels, which will in turn indirectly benefit your sleep.

Exercise Ideas

- Gym – This is my personal favourite, and the great feeling after a workout is almost addictive. Try to combine vigorous aerobic exercise with weights and aim to use all the muscles of your body. I go every other day and alternate this with some of the other sports listed below.

- Going for a jog – This is the best option if you don't want to spend anything. Combine it with a dog walk to kill two birds with one stone.

- Squash – The ultimate aerobic racket sport, a few games of squash provides an intense workout.

- Football, rugby, basketball, hockey, tennis, lacrosse, golf, athletics, swimming, rowing, cycling – All of these are perfect for getting your blood pumping.

Summary

- Exercise can have a markedly positive effect on your brain, your mood and your sleep.

- It's best to try to time the ending of your workout or

sports session for around 4 to 5 hours before you go to sleep, so between 6pm and 7pm.

Further Reading

- http://www.pnas.org/content/101/22/8473.long
- http://www.sciencedirect.com/science/article/pii/S0001691802001348

4. Simplifying Study

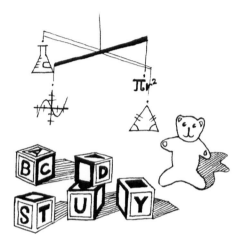

A vast amount has been written about how to study effectively. It could be argued that there's not one perfect system that will get you results every time, and that different subjects and difficulty levels of exams require a tailored approach. Moreover, many would contend that nobody is alike and that the way a person studies is unique to them. I believe that this is true, but only in part, since experimentation combined with the helpful advice of another friend has shown me that one particular study method seems to be especially appropriate in most scenarios. First, however, we need to consider how you should plan your study.

The Importance of a Study Timetable

A well thought out timetable provides a framework for your study and helps you to maintain a regular pattern of work and food. My advice on this front is simple – you should start early and finish early, allowing for breaks in between subjects and a longer break for lunch. Subjects should be studied each day in the chronological order in which you'll sit your exams. The amount of time that you give to each subject should reflect the importance and length of an exam. Above all, you shouldn't be working for any longer than five to six hours per day. Overleaf is an image showing the timetable that I used for the first set of exams in my second year at law school.

Revision Timetable

8:30 - 10:00   Property

Break

10:30 - 12:00   Civil Litigation

Break

12:15 - 1:15   Criminal Litigation

Nap or
Lunch

2:30 - 4:00   Business

Aim to do the following:

- Get out of bed at 7am and eat a wholesome breakfast

- Sit down to work at 8:30am

- Never spend more than 2 hours on a subject

- Never study for more than 2 hours at a time

- Only study for a maximum of 5 to 6 hours per day

- Take a 15 to 30 minute break in between sessions

- Only study a maximum of 4 to 5 subjects per day

I've found that when you're trying hard to absorb information, it becomes very difficult to concentrate for longer than two hours at a time, and taking a decent break in between intensive bouts of learning allows you to check your emails, have some food and relax your mind. The key theme here is therefore *quality* study for a *shorter* period of time and early in the day, as opposed to trying to force yourself to work for eight hours through the afternoon and late into the evening, which will only lead to frustration, poor concentration and a lack of worthwhile learning. Less really is more when it comes to exam preparation.

I've often heard people complaining that while they understand where I'm coming from with my suggestion that they work earlier in the day, they're just "the kind of person that works better later in the day". Since I know that some of you might be thinking along similar lines, I propose that you try to actively fight this instinct and here is why. If you've ever been attracted to this kind of study pattern when preparing for exams in the past, certain factors will quite possibly have been pushing you towards this way of working. I'm guessing that you probably go to bed too late, which means you'll get up late. The quality of your sleep will be affected, and you'll feel more tired in the morning, even if you think you've had a decent seven or eight hours' sleep. You'll eat a sub-standard breakfast bolstered by coffee which will start to wake you up, but then you'll remember those chores that you need to get done, and before you know it, lunchtime has come around. You'll then finally get down to doing some studying by 2pm, but already your body will be well past its optimum in terms of its capacity to learn and remember. Ultimately this vicious cycle will continue unchecked – that is, unless you do something about it.

By following my approach you won't need to be an

'afternoon worker' because you'll find it far easier to start your work early and with positive determination. You'll be particularly satisfied when, by late morning, you've already done four hours of work. You'll then enjoy your lunch knowing that you've only got an hour or two more to do in the afternoon. You'll be fully done by 4pm or earlier, safe in the knowledge that you've put in a focused shift with genuine results. Most importantly, you've then got the rest of the day to enjoy yourself, and this is the clincher – with my approach you've got the time to play sport, practise an instrument, go on a cinema date, or do whatever you want to do. By having this long period of free time to look forward to *every day*, it makes it *far* easier to sit down in the morning. I've also spoken to people who think for some reason that you shouldn't be having any fun during the period of exam preparation and that everything you do should be focused on your exams – what complete rubbish!

Weekends

Weekends are important because they give you something else to look forward to. The worst-case scenario is that you only have two weeks until your exams, in which case unfortunately you'll probably have to work both those weekends before your exams.

However, if for example you still have four weeks until your exams, then by all means treat three of the four weekends before those exams as half days by only working up until midday. You owe it to yourself, and there's nothing like having an incentive to work towards.

Study Leave & Studying after School or Work

Find out well in advance how much study leave you'll be given before your exams. This is crucial, since it determines your whole gameplan. For example, if you find that you're going to be given two weeks of study leave to prepare for eight GCSEs, this is clearly not enough time to study fully for those exams! If you find yourself confronted with a problem like this, I advise that you try to study for up to two hours after every school day for two to four weeks before your study leave begins. By starting slowly like this and getting your notes written well before your study leave, you should be able to build a strong foundation on which to base your learning when your study leave comes around.

Studying after school takes a great deal of commitment and is much more difficult to get yourself motivated for, since you may be in a bad mood, or simply feel that you can't take any more. Therefore, before sitting down to study, it's essential that you take a power nap (more on this later), drink lots of water, and eat some nutritious snacks such as nuts, blueberries or a banana. This should help you to get in the right frame of mind and prepare your body to push on for a couple of hours more, but only that.

Lastly, I'm well aware that people studying for certain professional qualifications such as the CFA, have to try to study after work when they can, which is one of the issues that makes preparing for exams such as these so demanding. My answer to this conundrum would be to start your studying many months in advance and to do just a little at a time when possible after work. That way you'll never feel overwhelmed by the amount of material that you have to learn and can take it at your own pace.

A Week-by-Week Approach

The number of weeks that you have to prepare for your exams will be the main factor in determining how you allot your time. On the following page are a number of different scenarios to try to show how I believe you might best spend that time.

2 weeks until exams

- Week 1 – writing notes 50% / learning 50%
- Week 2 – learning 50% / practice questions 50%

4 weeks until exams

- Week 1 – writing notes 100%
- Week 2 – learning 100%
- Week 3 – learning 50% / practice questions 50%
- Week 4 – learning 50% / practice questions 50%

6 weeks until exams

- Week 1 – writing notes 100%
- Week 2 – writing notes 100%
- Week 3 – learning 100%
- Week 4 – learning 100%
- Week 5 – learning 50% / practice questions 50%
- Week 6 – learning 50% / practice questions 50%

Be clear that this is only a guide and, if for example you have four weeks until your exams and need to spend eight days writing notes, then this isn't a problem. Simply adjust your schedule accordingly. Where an activity is listed as 50%, this means spending the first 45 minutes of a potential 90-minute subject slot on learning your notes, and the second 45 minutes on completing practice questions. It does *not* mean spending the first three hours of the day learning your notes and the second three hours of the day on practice questions! This would be tedious and might result in you preferring one half of the day to the other, which is something we're trying to avoid.

How Many Subjects per Day?

You'll have seen that my timetable above shows how I studied only four subjects per day for those exams. Trial and error has shown me that studying no more than four to five subjects per day seems to be the optimum – any more and you risk beginning to feel swamped. I recognize that many students will have significantly more subjects to study for at a given time – GCSEs in the UK being a good example. However, I still advise that you limit the number of subjects that you study per day. That way, given an absolute maximum of six hours' study time per day, you can then give each subject 60 to 90 minutes of focused attention.

If you do have more than five subjects to study for, then simply split your subjects into two groups that can be studied every other day. From experience, having an extra day in between studying subjects doesn't seem to alter the efficacy of your study. On the plus side, it actually makes studying less repetitive (which is always a good thing), and there have been certain findings to indicate that such a delay may in fact aid memory consolidation. Therefore, don't worry about this extra time in between, but do be mindful that you'll need to double the amount of time you spend studying, since four weeks spent studying a subject every other day is only the equivalent of two full weeks spent studying that subject!

The Miniaturised Notes Technique

Mind maps, study cards, dictaphone recordings, personalised online quizzes – you name it, I've tried it. There's no doubt that all of the above can be used effectively as study tools, but they all share one common problem – they take far too long to produce in the first place and you end up spending more time creating them than actually studying. By comparison, my miniaturised notes technique is deceptively simple, yet highly effective.

With six weeks to go until my first year legal exams in 2013, I set about writing my usual long-form notes. I calculated that with six different exams, each containing three different question topics, I could just about write all the notes that I required for the 18 different types of questions that I would need to answer, which would then leave me three further weeks to learn and practise the material. I did succeed in writing all those notes, but I counted them up at the end of an intense three weeks and found that I'd produced 280 sides of notes! I'd never had so much to learn and my response had been to go into note-making overdrive. I stared in despair and mounting panic at this great pile of pages, not knowing how on earth I'd learn it all.

That night I went to the gym and asked an old school friend (and probably the brightest guy I know) for some advice. He said that I should turn the notes that I'd already made into a quarter of the number. So I went away and reckoned that I could just about afford to spend a week miniaturising the notes that I'd already written. At the end of that week, whereas once I had 16 sides of notes per question topic, I now only had an average of four, which came to 72 sides overall – pretty bearable. I did this by making sure that I cut any irrelevant information and had just the bare bones and structure that I needed to adequately complete each question topic. I also wrote in smaller handwriting that enabled me to compress more words on to a page.

So the technique is this: you should aim to only produce a maximum of four sides of notes per major exam topic. Do this by keeping the detail of your notes very basic where possible (abbreviate, use arrows and symbols, and make up short phrases to describe ideas or processes with which you are already familiar). Above all, concentrate on creating notes based on the structure of the questions that you'll be answering.

The genius of making notes like this is that it's firstly psychologically easier to learn and remember a smaller number of notes overall and, secondly, it seems to be the case that because you're only dealing with a few sides per topic, it's possible with repeated study to create an image of those few sides in your mind. This will allow you to recall the information visually during an exam, even if like me you would in no way describe yourself as having a photographic memory! Experience of note writing in the past has shown me that this is much more difficult to do with lots of different pages of notes, and it seems to be that my friend was spot on when he inadvertently implied a four side maximum. And, lastly, the fact that you might have, as in my case,

18 different sets of four sides, doesn't seem to make a difference. The ease of learning appears to stem from grouping the topics into a maximum of four sides each.

I would wholeheartedly recommend *hand*writing your notes as opposed to typing them. I believe that the act of writing notes is a crucial first phase in the learning process, and each side of notes will be far more memorable in layout if handwritten, which should make it easier for you to visualise each side in your mind. Feel free to highlight, underline specific points or draw little pictures in your notes for emphasis once you've written them, but don't waste too much time doing this.

See overleaf one of the 72 sides of notes that I mention above. I've subsequently used this technique to great effect.

Tort — Occupier's Liability

= "Concerned with the state of the land"

OLA 1957

Who is the occupier? (s1(c) makes reference to common law)

- not defined in either Act, so we look to common law.
  Wheat v Lacon = "anyone with a sufficient degree of control over
  premises. Can be more than one (Collier v Anglian Water Authority).
- 'Independent contractors' can be occupiers too (AMF International v Magnet Bowling).
- Possible for occupier to be an absentee (Harris v Birkenhead Corp.).

Premises? (s1(3)(a) = identical in 1984 act also)

- "any fixed or moveable structure including any vessel, vehicle, aircraft."
- a ladder! (Wheeler v Copas)

Visitor?

- not defined, so we look to common law.
- Express permission a) Area = can be limited (The Calgarth)
                                    = subjective test, signs need to be understood, age
                                       needs to be taken into account (Pearson v Coleman Bros)
                            b) Time = Stone v Taffe
                            c) Purpose = R v Smith v Jones
- Implied permission = this exists due to an occupiers behaviour, eg = postman.
                          (Lowery v Walker)
- Lawful authority = s2(6) - eg. police officers w/ warrant etc (Ogwo v Taylor)
- Contractual Permission = s5(1) - implied terms under a contract ie d. of. c.
- Public/Private right of way = public - (Greenhalgh v BRB), private. (OLA Abby)

How to Learn Effectively

When I was around 11 years old, my school brought in a lady who spent a small amount of time with each student and who afterwards provided an analysis of what kind of approach to learning would be suitable for them, based on a series of tests. I was said to be a 'combo' learner, in other words somebody who learns best from both seeing and hearing material. The results of my classmates showed that the majority were similar to me. What I took away from this, and what science has proved, is that the more ways in which we stimulate our senses while learning, the better we absorb and remember information.

It follows that just silently reading your notes over and over again will *not* do. You have to animate and energise those words so that they stick in your mind. Use a combination of reading in your mind, reading out loud and, whenever you get the urge to fidget, get up with your notes and walk around. The act of walking around seems to stop any need to fidget and, before long, you'll be pacing around the room where you're studying, speaking out loud and getting positively energised by the words that you've written. You never know, you might enjoy yourself! Vary the tone of your voice and really try to concentrate on projecting the words on the page into your mind as an image. If you need to, try thinking of images in your mind that reflect not just the layout of the words on the page, but also any images associated with the words. If you're worried that your family or friends will think you've gone mad, then simply tell them that you'll be speaking out loud and walking around the room where you're studying, and that there's nothing to worry about!

On your first day of learning the notes that you've made, you'll probably find it fairly difficult to get them to instantly stick in your mind. Don't worry, because even if you don't think that you're remembering anything, your brain is soaking up the information and starting to piece it together. Finish your day's studying, get some sleep, and return to your learning the following day. Then, as discussed in 'The Power of Sleep', you'll almost certainly find that, perhaps surprisingly, you do in fact now remember some or possibly quite a lot of what you studied the previous day. Keep on repeating this process of going over material and sleeping on it. Within about five to ten days the information will start to become ingrained and, after two weeks, I find that you can begin to visualise the exact page of notes in your mind. This would be the earliest you could sit an exam, and you would probably do well in it. If, however, you have the luxury of four weeks or more to prepare, then by the time your exams come around, you'll very likely be almost able to recite your notes by heart. By combining the different elements of sleep, food, exercise and the approach to exam preparation that I propose, I think you'll be truly amazed at your increased ability to take in information.

Past Papers & Practice Questions

When I was younger I used to have a foolish notion that past papers were an unnecessary effort and to be avoided. How wrong I was. Past papers are absolutely vital to your success and also take on additional value when practised under exam conditions, which I would strongly recommend. Thinking back to GCSEs and beyond, I don't think there has ever been an exam that I was due to sit where some sort of past paper or practice question wasn't accessible beforehand. They are almost universally available in the run up to all exams and, if your teacher/tutor has not provided any, then enquire as to why and try to get your hands on as many as possible. Past papers and/or practice questions are vital for the following reasons:

- Firstly, they allow you to test your knowledge and check for any gaps in your understanding of a topic.

- Secondly, they allow you to see what topics are more likely to come up in an exam, and the types of questions that an examiner will be likely to set you. This element is particularly crucial, and I advise that you actively consult past papers on a question topic before even starting to write your notes so that you're in the best possible position to understand how a question needs to be answered, and so that you can tailor your notes accordingly. If there are any model answers available, so much the better.

- Thirdly, they allow you to work out in advance the exact amount of time that you should be spending relative to the number of marks available on a particular question. More on this later.

Where to Study

If you try to use the techniques of reading your notes out loud and walking around, this will almost certainly be frowned upon in your school or university's library, where silence reigns supreme. There's nothing wrong with *writing* notes in a room like this, but when it comes to learning the material, I recommend that you find an unused classroom or lecture room – just ask the person in charge and I'm certain that they'll be happy for you to use one of these rooms. I myself am a big fan of working in a quiet room at home, so this is another option.

Wherever you do choose to work, make sure that your phone is silenced (no vibrate function either) and that, if there's a PC or laptop in the room, it's *fully* switched off. Choose a well-lit room with both natural and artificial light and a good airflow – open windows are far preferable to air-conditioning that will likely dry out your eyes and may cause a stuffy nose (speaking from experience).

Music

In recent times this has been less of a theme, but when I was younger I used to frequently see friends listening to music while studying. If you're trying to focus all your energy on learning material, then I can't help feeling that listening to music while doing so must have an adverse effect and, what's more, it seems entirely incompatible with the way that I'm suggesting you learn. So I recommend that you avoid music while learning, and also equally while writing notes. The act of writing notes should be one of quiet concentration that should help create a first image of the words in your mind. Don't ruin this concentration with lyrics and music in your ears!

Music does, however, have a potential role to play in your exam preparation. I suggest that you choose a 'study tune' to start every day with. It needs to be a track that you'll listen to once before you begin your work each day, and one that will give you a boost and signal that it's time to confront the day head on. It can be something corny like 'Eye of the Tiger' by Survivor, or something rousing like 'Desert Song' by Edward Sharpe and the Magnetic Zeros. It doesn't matter whether your thing is rock, reggae, classical etc., but simply that you choose a tune which inspires you.

Power Naps

You may have noticed that in the example of my own study timetable above, there's a period labelled 'Nap'. We've already seen how sleep has the capacity to affect your mood, stress and memory, and a 'power nap' is no different. From a combination of my own experience and evidence provided by numerous scientific studies, power naps work best if 20 to 30 minutes long, but no longer. The key is not to actually fall into a deep sleep, since to do so will make you feel groggy when you wake. Instead, lie down in a dark room, close your eyes and clear your mind of all thoughts. Breathe deeply and relax your body completely. After 20 to 30 minutes you'll probably be near to sleep or lightly dozing. This is the point when the alarm that you'll have set will go off and it'll be time to get up. Once you've snapped out of a slight haze, you'll feel truly re-energised. For obvious reasons, studying at home or in a university room is recommended to allow you to power nap with ease.

Studies by many diverse institutions from NASA to a number of universities have shown the benefits of power naps as being the same as that of regular sleep. A power nap will help to reduce stress and simultaneously boost memory and cognitive function. I would therefore strongly suggest a power nap late in the morning after perhaps four hours of work. This will help your brain to consolidate those memories that you've already formed, reduce any stress that has built up over the morning, and sharpen your concentration and alertness in preparation for the final push through lunch and into the afternoon.

As a word of advice, you might be tempted to take a power nap after lunch, but a full stomach seems to precipitate sleep much more quickly and, since we're trying to prevent deep sleep, this should be avoided.

Summary

- Draw up an easy to follow study timetable and stick to it, keeping to the rules outlined above.

- Use enjoyable activities planned for afternoons and weekends as valuable incentives to get your work done in good time.

- Determine how many weeks of study leave you have until your exams and apply an appropriate strategy as outlined above.

- Miniaturise your notes into a maximum of 4 sides (2 pages) per major exam topic by only writing down a basic structure containing the information that you really need and by writing in a smaller script.

- Learn your notes with energy. Read silently and aloud, and walk around while doing both. Vary the tone of your voice and try to visually transfer the words from the page into your mind. The process of absorption is gradual and closely linked to sleep. If you create the environment for this to happen, results *will* follow.

- Past papers and practice questions are your best friend. Use them every day under exam conditions in the later stages of your exam preparation.

- Choose a suitable location in which to work. I believe that your own room at home or university is always preferable when it comes to learning notes.

- Don't listen to music while writing or learning notes. Do, however, listen to a study tune just before starting a day's work.

- Power naps are your secret weapon. Take them every day and experiment to find the exact length of nap that works for you.

Further Reading

- http://sleepfoundation.org

5. Exams: Zero Hour

You've closely followed everything that I've suggested and now the day before your first exam has finally arrived. Unlike many of your friends who'll be frantically cramming, hoping that they'll be able to remember the different stages of cellular respiration or how to solve a quadratic equation, you should be quietly content in the knowledge that you've planned well in advance and absorbed more information than you ever thought possible.

At this point you should remain calm and run through your notes one more time during the morning. You shouldn't be doing any more practice questions on this final day, unless of course you've only had a couple of weeks to prepare and are still completing your timetable. Take the whole afternoon off to exercise. This will help you to relax, prepare you for a very good night's sleep and provide your brain with much needed oxygen.

Make sure that you know the address of the exam venue (carefully check your travel plans for possible public transport strikes etc.), the timing of the exam, and how long before the exam you are expected to arrive – then print off a map. You never know when the sat nav on your phone might fail you. You should aim to be in bed by 10pm or earlier.

If you think all of this sounds like a military operation then you've got the right idea. Planning ahead is vital and eliminates stressful situations.

Exam Day

On the day of an exam, I recommend getting up around three to four hours before a morning exam. For example, the final legal exams that I sat in mid-2014 started at 10:30am, so I would get up at 6:30am. Being a slow riser, this meant that I was downstairs by 7:15am. I would then spend one hour running through the notes of the exam that I'd be sitting to refresh my memory.

This was followed by the same wholesome breakfast as usual, and I was ready to leave the house by about 8:45am, giving me lots of time to get to the location of the exam 45 minutes away (if you're worried that the exam venue will be difficult to find, leave extra time to find it). I would finally arrive around 9:30am, which would mean that I would have a further hour until the exam started. No rush, no stress.

For an afternoon exam, start the day as you would on any other day that you've spent studying by running through your notes during the morning and finishing up with a power nap. Follow this with an early lunch that's both light and nutritious, then make your way in good time to the exam venue.

On arriving at the venue, greet your friends, but thereafter avoid talking to others who'll most likely be excitable and/or worried. During the hour before the exam begins, I suggest that you just sit, close your eyes and breathe deeply, or possibly have a swift read through any specific notes if you need a quick refresher. When you're called, walk calmly into the room and, if you have a choice of desk, find one that has either a good artificial light source above it or which is near to a window. If possible, sit near or at the front of the room, where there's less distraction from people sitting ahead of you. Here it may also be easier to hear the exam invigilator speak, and to see a clock if you haven't been allowed to bring one yourself.

Hydration

On the day of an exam you should drink a few glasses of water in the morning when you get up to re-hydrate your body and brain. Make sure you hydrate during the morning in the run up to an exam, but don't drink too much in the hour before, since this could lead to your needing breaks later on. The key is to take a comfort break just before the start of an exam, then to take little sips of water throughout the exam. This will allow you to remain hydrated up to and during an exam, but should avoid the need for any breaks taking up valuable exam time. However, if you do need to go, go! There's nothing worse than trying to answer a question when you're desperate and it will destroy your concentration.

What to Wear

What you wear during an exam can significantly impact upon your level of personal comfort. If you have a choice and are not confined to wearing a school uniform, try to wear clothes which are loose fitting and in which you feel completely comfortable. The temperature of an exam room can vary dramatically in my experience. If you find that the temperature of the room is a problem, you must absolutely ask the exam invigilator to do what they can to change it – you're almost certainly not alone in your discomfort. To prepare for any eventuality, take a variety of layers in case temperature problems persist.

Choice of Exam Pen

An often-overlooked area of discussion is your choice of exam pen, which should be another weapon in your arsenal for getting one-up on your peers. Go to your local stationer and try out as many pens as possible. Find the type of pen that feels right for you. I've found that gel pens with a consistent ink flow and a medium-narrow nib are best. Avoid fountain pens and biros, the former having too much potential for an explosion and the latter requiring that you press too hard on the page, tiring your arm. One final consideration is the size of grip. I would recommend a slightly wider diameter, rubbery grip. When we're writing fast and under time pressure, we tend to grip our pens fairly tightly. A narrow, firm plastic grip appears to exacerbate this problem, leading to the potential for finger strain and/ or hand cramp, whereas a wider rubbery grip seems to help.

Your Exam Toolkit

The following is a list of the essential items that you should always have with you in an exam:

- Digital clock (silent, with no beeps or vibrations)
- Bottle of water
- Highlighters
- Exam pens
- Spare exam pens of the same type as those that you intend to use to write in the exam

I find that a digital clock is much easier to read quickly and more accurately when you're under pressure and, by having your own clock on your desk, it's simple to glance up from your work and have a quick time check whenever you need it. The reason for a bottle of water should be obvious by now. And lastly, highlighters are especially useful for highlighting the crucial words in a question.

Exam Tactics

The most difficult thing about this chapter is that although I believe I can have a significant impact on how you prepare for your exams, there's less I can do once you're in an exam room. Exam taking is an art, and some people are better at it than others. I make no claim to being a master taker of exams, but what I have found is that you can sway the odds in your favour by having a plan and sticking to it. I propose that you closely follow the tips below to give yourself the best possible chance of success:

- Eat a banana 30 minutes before going into an exam. This will give you an energy boost and prepare you for the task ahead. Snack on unsalted nuts during an exam when necessary, but only if this won't slow you down or annoy others. For especially long exams, eat another banana half way through.

- As already touched upon, use past papers to work out in advance of an exam how many minutes per mark you should allow yourself, but make sure that you factor in enough reading time. So, for a 3 hour exam (180 minutes) with 100 marks available, start by working out that this is 1.8 minutes per mark (i.e. 1 minute 48 seconds). You then need to factor in reading time. Don't get too bogged down in any complicated maths by trying to work out exactly how many seconds of reading time to give yourself per mark. Instead, just round the amount of time you have to do the question down a bit. In this example, 1.5 minutes per mark (i.e. 1 minute 30 seconds) would seem appropriate and, if you end up spending less time reading than you've planned for, you'll simply have more time to check your answers at the end. Therefore, this would mean that you would have 15 minutes to do a 10 mark question (not including 3 minutes for reading the question). Go into an exam knowing how much time you have and stick to your plan.

- Find out exactly what the question is asking of you. Highlight the key words and read a question two or three times if you have to and feel no shame in doing so – being under pressure can make even the most simple question appear complicated.

- Plan your answers for longer questions on a piece of rough paper. However, keep your plan very basic and don't waste time on too much detail – remember that anything you write on rough paper will usually *not* be marked.

- You don't necessarily have to answer the questions in the order that they're set, and don't be scared of answering an exam in a way that suits *you*. For example, if you intend to begin with question 2 and then do question 1, this isn't a problem, but make this *very* obvious to the examiner on your exam writing paper or booklet.

- Don't panic! If you're struggling on a question, chances are that others will be too, so move on, leave a suitable amount of space or pages free to allow you to come back and answer the question later, and then tackle the next question.

- If you're finding it difficult to stick to the timings per question that you calculated before going into an exam, assess the situation rationally. If you're slowing down because you have too much to say and can't get it all down quickly enough, then focus on simplifying your answer and moving on to the next question as quickly as possible. If, on the other hand, you're getting behind because you're finding the question difficult to answer and it's holding you back, stop answering the question immediately and move on to the next question. In other words, it's far better to lose 5 marks on a question than to waste 25 minutes of valuable time trying in vain to answer it.

- Use all the time that you have available at the end of an exam (if any) to check your answers and NEVER leave early. You might feel a bit silly if everyone else has left the room while you're still sitting there with 30 minutes to go, but when you find a spelling mistake on the fourth re-read of your answers, it *will* be worth it.

I've now given you the information necessary to make a real difference to the way in which you approach study and exams. The potential to improve your grades is in your hands and it's up to you to put everything that I've recommended into practice.

GOOD LUCK!

Summary

- Get up 3 to 4 hours before a morning exam and do a full run through your notes before having a wholesome breakfast as usual. For an afternoon exam, get up at your regular time and spend a couple of hours going over your notes during the morning. Follow this with a power nap, and then have a light, nutritious lunch.

- Hydrate continually in the lead up to an exam, but ease off in the hour before.

- Arrive 1 hour before an exam with your exam toolkit, avoid talking to others and remain calm.

- Eat a banana 30 minutes before going into an exam and snack on unsalted nuts and another banana where necessary during an exam.

- Take a comfort break immediately before an exam.

- If you have a choice, choose a desk at the front of the exam room with good lighting.

- Stick to your exam tactics by following the timing schedule that you've prepared and by reading each question particularly carefully.

- If you get stuck on a question, leave enough space to answer it later and move on to another question.

- If you find that you're not keeping to the timings that you've set yourself per question, assess the situation calmly and act accordingly as outlined above.

- NEVER leave an exam early! Just keep re-reading your answers.

Afterthoughts & Observations

I decided to finally write this book after my first year of law school. I had been shocked by my peers' approach to exams at school and university, and tales of late night study sessions fuelled by caffeine and sweets made me realize that there was without doubt scope for development in this area. In addition, it had come to my attention that, although there was a significant amount of information out there on how to eat healthily, get better sleep, study more intelligently etc., nobody had yet combined all these elements and shown both how closely linked they all are and also how with quick adjustments to your lifestyle, it's easy to see visible results in a matter of days. The science was there to support it, but somehow this area had gone unchecked.

So, when my first year legal exams came around, it was the first time in a couple of years that I was now both able to fully put my newly developed ideas into practice and also see the results. By the end of my second year of law school I had tweaked and refined my approach. With exams throughout the past year (at the time of writing), there has been ample opportunity to continue putting my theories into practice. I've been stunned by the positive effect that my strategy has had on my body, brain and ultimately my grades, with which

I was delighted. I never believed that relatively simple lifestyle changes could have such a profound effect on my concentration and enable me to absorb a much greater amount of information than I had ever thought possible. Now I hope that you too can benefit from the strategy that I've perfected and discover that the Holy Grail of exam success is within your reach.

As a final observation, you may well find that once you've spent a certain amount of time following what I propose in terms of sleep, food and exercise, that you may actually never want to revert to your old ways. Not only will you feel great, but you could also see some additional positive side effects. I've noted that these can include improved happiness as a result of a more balanced mood, weight loss, and possibly increased immunity. The latter is, though, more difficult for me to prove scientifically! Yes, it will require willpower on your part to change lifestyle habits that are possibly deeply ingrained. However, please try to follow *all* of my suggestions. In the academically dependent job market in which you'll most likely compete, the best results will, without a shadow of doubt, be well worth the extra effort.

Notes

Notes

Notes

Notes

Notes